WILD·WORLD·OF·ANIMALS

FORESTS

MICHAEL CHINERY
ILLUSTRATED BY BERNARD LONG
AND ERIC ROBSON

Kingfisher Books

Kingfisher Books, Grisewood & Dempsey Ltd,
Elsley House, 24–30 Great Titchfield Street,
London W1P 7AD

First published in 1992 by Kingfisher Books
10 9 8 7 6 5 4 3 2 1

BRITISH LIBRARY CATALOGUING-IN-PUBLICATION DATA
A catalogue record for this book is available from
the British Library

ISBN 0 86272 915 7

Series editor: Mike Halson
Series designer: Terry Woodley
Designer: Dave West Children's Books
Illustrators: Michael Gaffney/*Garden Studio* (p. 12, 28);
Bernard Long/*Temple Rogers* (pp. 1–3, 8–11, 14–15,
19–21, 25, 29, 32–33, 36–37); Eric Robson/*Garden Studio*
(p. 4–7, 13, 16–18, 22–24, 26–27, 30–31, 34–35, 38)
Cover illustrations: John Butler

Phototypeset by Southern Positives and Negatives
(SPAN), Lingfield, Surrey.
Printed and bound by Cambus Litho Ltd, East Kilbride.

Contents

Life in the forests

The animals in this book all live in the cooler parts of the world, where there are two very different types of woodlands. Deciduous woodlands are made up of trees that drop their leaves for the winter, while evergreen woods stay green all year. The woodland plants provide food and shelter for a fantastic variety of animals, from tiny insects to the magnificent moose. Most of them eat leaves and seeds, but there are also lots of insect-eating birds and other meat-eating animals in the woodlands.

Here you can see some of the huge variety of animals that inhabit deciduous woodlands. Animals in the forest live at all levels, from below the ground up to the tops of the tallest trees.

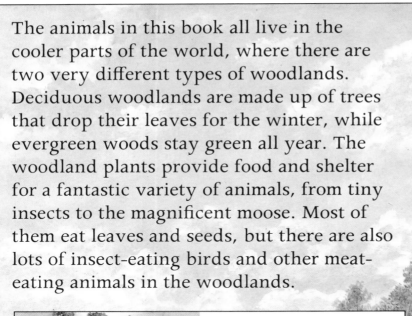

EVERGREENS

Evergreen woodlands usually grow in colder places than deciduous woods. They consist mainly of pines, firs and other cone-bearing trees with tough needle-like leaves, and have less animal life than deciduous woodlands.

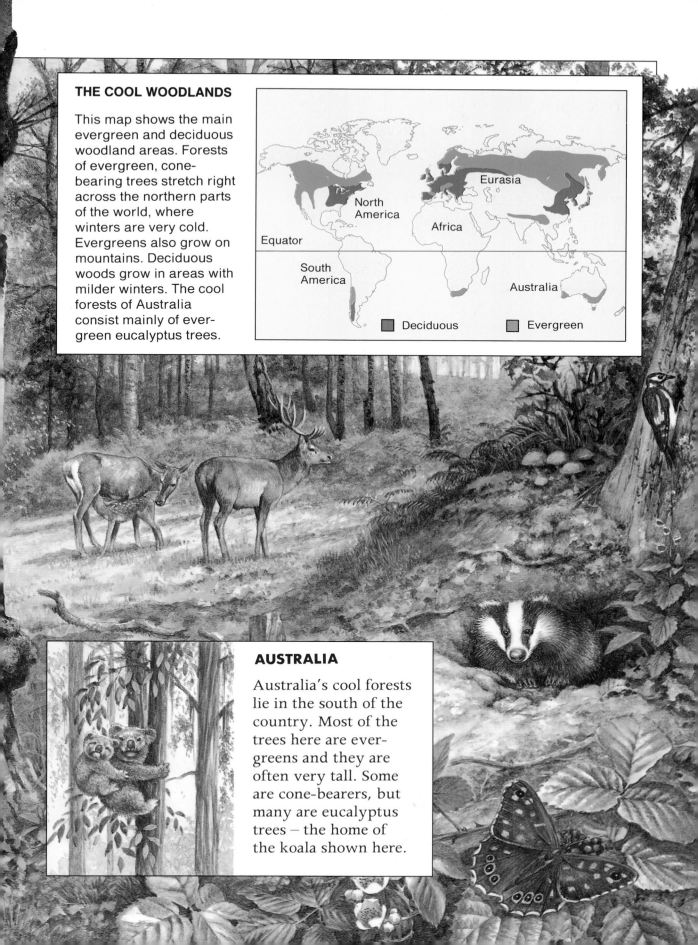

THE COOL WOODLANDS

This map shows the main evergreen and deciduous woodland areas. Forests of evergreen, cone-bearing trees stretch right across the northern parts of the world, where winters are very cold. Evergreens also grow on mountains. Deciduous woods grow in areas with milder winters. The cool forests of Australia consist mainly of evergreen eucalyptus trees.

Eurasia

North America

Africa

Equator

South America

Australia

■ Deciduous   ■ Evergreen

AUSTRALIA

Australia's cool forests lie in the south of the country. Most of the trees here are evergreens and they are often very tall. Some are cone-bearers, but many are eucalyptus trees – the home of the koala shown here.

The badger

The European badger lives in deciduous woodlands all over Europe and in much of Asia. It is a sturdy, dog-sized animal with strong, short legs that are ideal for digging. It lives in a family group in an underground home called a sett, in which it makes a comfortable bed with dried grass and leaves. Badgers come out at night and eat almost anything, but earthworms are their most important food.

BADGER FACTS

● The male badger is called a boar and the female is called a sow. Each may weigh up to 17 kg.

● American badgers live on the prairies, not in the woods.

Badgers often scratch tree trunks with their front feet. This may be a way of marking out their home territory with scent.

The badger's stripes help to camouflage it by breaking up the outline of its head. This works especially well at night.

Badgers regularly clean their setts, taking the old bedding out and replacing it with a fresh supply of grass and leaves.

Hundreds of badgers are killed every year trying to cross busy roads. The problem has been partly solved by building special tunnels under roads so that the badgers can cross in safety.

Badgers never dirty their homes with their droppings. Each family digs itself a special toilet pit.

Badgers sometimes set off after rabbits, but they are far too slow to catch them.

A BADGER SETT

A sett has many rooms linked by a maze of corridors. The sett may be passed from one generation to the next over several decades.

Room used during birth of cubs

Sleeping room

Bedding

The pine processionary

The pine processionary is a European moth that gets its name because its caterpillars walk in long lines or processions. They live in large groups in pine trees and each group makes a nest of silk. The caterpillars spend the day in the nest and go out to nibble the pine needles at night. Each caterpillar touches the one in front as the procession moves from the nest to feed in the surrounding branches.

The silk nest is home to hundreds of pine processionary caterpillars. It may be the size of a rugby ball.

The caterpillars feed on pine needles. This can kill the trees and cause serious harm to the forests.

? DO YOU KNOW

The caterpillars sleep in their nests all winter. In the spring they burrow in the ground and turn into chrysalises. Adult moths like this one emerge in the summer.

The caterpillars are protected by poison-tipped hairs that cause pain to any animal that touches them.

Battling stag beetles

Stag beetles get their name because the males' jaws are like stags' antlers. They fight with their antlers and the strongest males get to mate with the females.

Stag beetles live in many of the world's woodlands. These wrestling European stag beetles are 5 cm long.

SURVIVAL WATCH

Stag beetles grow up in tree stumps, feeding on the rotting wood. European stag beetles are becoming rare because foresters clear away the dead wood that the beetles need.

The fiery wood ant

Wood ants build large nests on the woodland floor and cover them with pine needles and other leaves. Many thousands of ants live in each nest.

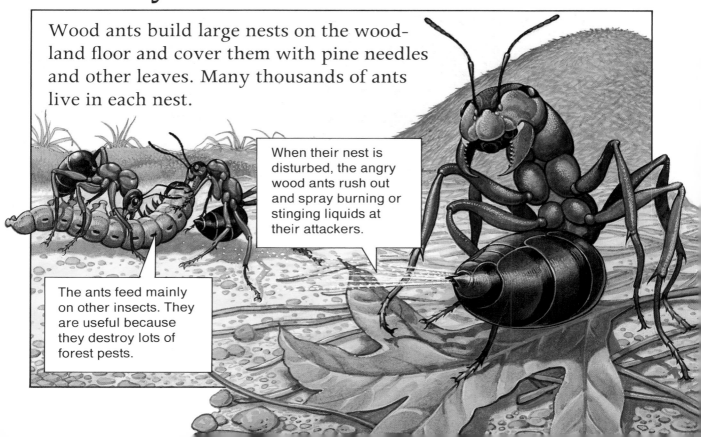

When their nest is disturbed, the angry wood ants rush out and spray burning or stinging liquids at their attackers.

The ants feed mainly on other insects. They are useful because they destroy lots of forest pests.

The noisy jay

The Eurasian jay shown here lives in the woodlands of Europe and Asia, from the British Isles to Japan, but it is heard more than it is seen. When it is alarmed it utters piercing calls – *crar-crar-crar* – and flies off to a safer spot. Jays eat seeds, berries, and insects. They also steal and eat eggs and nestlings from the nests of other birds.

Jays are especially fond of acorns and are able to carry six or seven of them in their mouths at the same time.

? DO YOU KNOW

Jays often sit on ant nests and spread their wings. The angry ants crawl all over the birds, spraying acid as they go. But this is just what the jay wants. The spray kills the lice and fleas living among its feathers.

Jays bury a lot of their acorns. They don't always manage to find them again and the acorns may grow into new trees.

JAY FACTS

● The Eurasian jay is about 35 cm long. It can mimic many other bird calls and even copy human voices.

● Jays belong to the crow family. There are over 30 kinds, mostly in South America.

The nimble treecreeper

The treecreeper climbs up tree trunks in a spiral or zig-zag fashion as it looks for food. When it reaches the top of a trunk it flies to the base of another tree and starts to climb again. It cannot climb downwards.

Treecreepers live in the forests of the Northern Hemisphere. They usually build their nests behind loose bark or amongst the ivy growing on the trees.

The treecreeper's slender, curved beak is just right for getting at insects hiding in cracks in the bark.

The acrobatic nuthatch

The Eurasian nuthatch dashes about on tree trunks but, unlike the treecreeper, it can go down as well as up. It can even run down headfirst. It eats seeds as well as insects. The nuthatch nests in tree holes and often plasters the entrance with mud.

? DO YOU KNOW

The nuthatch gets its name from its habit of wedging nuts into gaps in the bark and then hitting the nuts with its sturdy beak until they crack open.

The pointed beak is perfect for picking up insects and also for breaking nuts.

The giant panda

The giant panda lives in the bamboo forests in the mountains of China. These cold forests are difficult to explore, so few people have ever seen wild pandas. Until 1869, no one outside China had even heard of the giant panda. We still do not know very much about its life in the wild. It feeds mainly on bamboo shoots, but it eats many other plants as well.

 GIANT PANDA FACTS

● The giant panda is up to 2 metres long and weighs 130 kg. It spends 10–12 hours of every day eating.

● The panda looks like a bear, but is more closely related to the raccoon (see page 24).

 SURVIVAL WATCH

The giant panda is very rare, but it is probably the most famous animal of all. It is the symbol of the World Wide Fund for Nature, a body that raises money to save animals and plants from extinction. The few wild pandas that are left are protected in nature reserves.

The panda has an extra thumb-like pad on its hand. This helps it to hold the bamboo shoots firmly while it chews them.

Female pandas have either one or two babies. They are very small at first, but put on 500 grams a week and grow quickly.

The speedy sparrowhawk

Sparrowhawks live in the forests of Eurasia and chase smaller birds through the trees at speeds up to 40 km/h. They flap their wings occasionally but glide for much of the time and make some incredibly tight turns as they dart between the trees. Their prey is usually snatched in mid-air and killed by the hawks' needle-sharp talons.

With its broad wings and long tail the sparrowhawk is ideally built for fast chases and rapid changes of direction.

SPARROWHAWK FACTS

● The male sparrow-hawk is 30 cm long and weighs 150 grams. The female is bigger and weighs 300 grams.

● Sparrowhawks pull the feathers off their prey before starting to eat them.

The curious kiwi

The kiwi lives only in New Zealand. It looks a bit like a long-beaked chicken, but it has no tail and it cannot fly. Its tiny wings are completely hidden among the hair-like feathers. Kiwis are shy birds that live mainly in the fern-filled forests. They sleep in burrows by day and come out to feed at night. They eat worms and insects living in the soil or among the dead leaves, and also enjoy fallen fruit.

SURVIVAL WATCH

Kiwis are becoming rare, largely because so many have been killed by the cats, dogs and other animals that people have taken to New Zealand.

The kiwi is a very strange-looking bird. Its dark coat looks more like shaggy hair than feathers.

KIWI FACTS

● The kiwi is up to 45 cm long, including its beak. It gets its name from its call of *ki-wee*.

● The female weighs only 4 kg, but she can lay two eggs weighing about 500 grams each – that's nearly ten times as heavy as a chicken's egg.

The nostrils at the tip of the beak can smell worms and other food several centimetres below the ground.

14

The brush-tailed possum

The brush-tailed possum looks like a fox and behaves like a monkey, but it is not related to either. It is Australia's commonest marsupial, or pouched mammal. It spends the daytime asleep in tree holes or in old rabbit burrows and comes out to feed at night. Tree buds and flowers are its favourite foods.

The female possum has one baby at a time. It rides on her back for about three months after leaving her pouch.

DO YOU KNOW

A few possums were taken to New Zealand in 1858. There are now millions of them there because they have no enemies.

Possums often cross roads at night. Their eyes shine brightly when they are picked up in car headlights.

The possum can wrap its furry tail around branches and use it like an extra arm or leg while climbing through the trees.

The cuddly koala

The koala is sometimes called the koala bear, but it is not a bear at all. Like the possum and the kangaroo, it is an Australian marsupial. Koalas weigh up to 15 kg and spend their lives climbing in the eucalyptus trees. Strong claws and special fingers help them to cling to the smoothest trunks and branches. They feed entirely on the eucalyptus leaves and hardly ever come down to the ground. A newly born koala is under 2 cm long and lives in its mother's pouch until it is six months old.

DO YOU KNOW

Koalas seem to snore and belch as they move about, but this is just their way of talking to each other.

Koalas live only in the eucalyptus forests of eastern Australia. Those living in the cooler, southern areas are larger than those from northern areas.

Two of the koala's five fingers go one way and the rest go the other, giving the koala a very good grip on the branches.

The female koala has only one baby at a time. The baby rides on her back for about a year after leaving her pouch.

Koalas living in the north-eastern part of Australia have silvery grey fur, but those from further south are much browner.

Koalas are not very active. They spend much of the daytime asleep, usually in the fork of a tree.

A koala eats about 1 kg of eucalyptus leaves a day. It does not drink because the leaves provide all the water it needs.

SURVIVAL WATCH

In the past, thousands of koalas were killed for their fur. This has been stopped, but koalas are still not safe because their forest homes are being cut down to make way for farms. Many koalas also die from diseases, although drugs are helping to bring these under control.

The wildcat

The wildcat is not just a cat that has gone wild. It is a true wild animal, living in the forests of Eurasia. It is very like a domestic tabby cat, but usually much larger, and its thick tail has very obvious black tail bands. The wildcat is a great hunter, creeping slowly up on its prey and then pouncing on it. Rabbits and rodents are its main foods, but it also catches fish, birds and insects.

? DO YOU KNOW

The first domestic cats lived in Egypt nearly 4000 years ago. They slowly spread into Europe and mated with wildcats. Our pet cats today are a mixture of African cats and European wildcats.

A cornered wildcat spits and snarls and fluffs up its fur to frighten its enemies. It actually prefers to run away than to fight.

A female teaches her kittens to pounce on prey by encouraging them to leap on her tail as she flicks it from side to side.

The wild boar

The wild boar is a wild pig that lives in the deciduous forests of Europe and Asia. It feeds mainly at night and eats almost anything it can find, including worms, insects, and mice. But plants are its main food. It digs for bulbs and underground fungi with its snout and feet, and in the autumn it grows fat on acorns and other types of nuts.

WILD BOAR FACTS

● Wild boar are up to 180 cm long and are about 100 cm high at the shoulder. They can weigh nearly 200 kg.

● Wild boar are usually rather shy, but the males sometimes attack when they are annoyed. They can do a lot of damage with their tusks.

? DO YOU KNOW

The wild boar is the ancestor of our farmyard pigs. The animals were first domesticated about 7000 years ago and there are now many different breeds. Pigs are much less hairy than the wild boar.

Wild boar females live with their piglets in small family groups. Males usually live alone, except in the winter mating season.

Wild boar have up to ten piglets in a litter. Their striped coats help to camouflage the piglets on the forest floor.

The boar's snout has a very good sense of smell. It is also tough enough to root about among the rubbish on the ground for food.

The mighty moose

The moose, or elk, lives in northern woodlands, especially in areas with plenty of lakes and rivers. In the winter it feeds mainly on the shoots, leaves and bark of willows and poplars. In the summer it rips up great mouthfuls of water lilies and other water plants. The males, or bulls, bellow loudly to attract the females in the autumn. The females usually give birth to twin babies in the summer.

MOOSE FACTS

● The moose is the world's biggest deer. Weighing as much as 850 kg, it is well over 2 metres high at the shoulder.

● Its coat is brown in the summer and grey in the winter.

The female moose is called a cow. She has no antlers. Females and males both have a prominent hump on the shoulders.

The male's antlers are up to 2 metres across. They fall off in December and new ones grow during the following summer.

During the summer the moose spend much of their time in the water, often with just their heads above the surface.

The wrestling red deer

Red deer live in the deciduous forests of Eurasia and also on the heather-covered moors of northern Britain. They feed on all kinds of plants. Only the males, called stags, have antlers. The antlers fall off in the spring, but new ones grow quickly in the summer. During the autumn mating season the stags get very noisy as they wrestle with each other and try to round up the females.

RED DEER FACTS

● Red deer become greyer in the autumn.

● Stags reach 150 cm high at the shoulder.

● A very similar deer, called a wapiti, lives in North America.

Deer shape the trees by nibbling the twigs and leaves. The line is at the height of the tallest deer.

The red deer always has a yellowish rump. Other large deer have white rumps, often with black marks.

Stags' antlers can measure 140 cm and weigh 6 kg each. The strongest stags have over 12 branches on each antler.

The Tasmanian devil

This dog-like animal is an Australian marsupial that lives in the eucalyptus woods. It eats all kinds of woodland animals, but, just like the hyaenas of Africa, it feeds mainly on creatures that are already dead.

 DEVIL FACTS

● The Tasmanian devil lives only in Tasmania – the large island off the south of Australia.

● Up to 1 metre long, including its tail, it is the largest surviving flesh-eating marsupial.

Tasmanian devils often fight each other and many have torn ears and other scars. But, despite their ferocious growls and fierce looks, they are not dangerous to people.

The gentle numbat

The numbat is one of Australia's rarest animals. Special efforts are being made to protect it in the woodlands in the south-west of the country. It feeds on termites, which it finds with its keen sense of smell.

The numbat opens up termite nests and tunnels with its claws and then mops up the insects with its long, sticky tongue.

The spiny porcupine

Porcupines are well protected by sharp spines or quills, which are made from special hairs. Some ground-living porcupines have quills over 30 cm long. The one shown here is the Canadian porcupine, a tree-living species from North America. It is about 1 metre long, including its tail. All porcupines belong to the group of gnawing mammals called rodents.

? DO YOU KNOW

The puma is the Canadian porcupine's main enemy, but the porcupine can defend itself well by lashing out with its spiny tail. The barbed quills then break loose and stick into the puma's flesh.

The porcupine's long fur hides more than 20,000 short, but very sharp spines that protect it from most other animals.

The short, spiny tail is a very good weapon, but it is unable to grip the branches like the long tails of South American porcupines.

The porcupine feeds at dawn and dusk. It mainly eats buds and bark, which it gnaws off with its sharp, chisel-like front teeth.

The furry raccoon

The North American raccoon, often called a coon, has striking black patches on its face like a burglar's mask. It is a skilful climber and in the spring it feeds largely on the eggs and chicks of small birds. It also eats worms and insects and is fond of corn on the cob. Many raccoons live in towns, where they find plenty of food in rubbish bins.

Raccoons are very good swimmers. They catch and eat quite a lot of fish, frogs, and other water-living animals.

RACCOON FACTS

● Raccoons are up to 1 metre long, including the tail. They weigh up to 20 kg.

● Raccoon skins used to be made into coats and other clothes. At one time they were even used as money.

With their five long fingers, the raccoon's front paws are ideal both for climbing and for picking up and holding food.

The stinking skunk

Not many animals dare to attack a skunk. When another animal gets too close, the skunk squirts it with a really awful-smelling liquid and the smell takes days to go away. The striped skunk shown here lives in the forests of North America. It is a cat-sized animal and it eats small animals, birds' eggs and fruit.

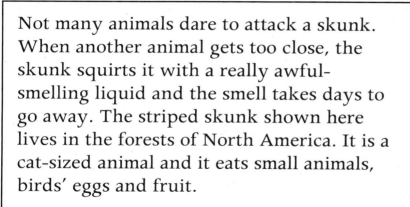

The stinking liquid jet is fired from glands under the skunk's tail and can travel as much as 3 metres.

This lynx is in for a nasty shock as the frightened skunk lifts its rear end ready to fend off an attack.

The skunk's long outer hairs are very coarse, but its soft underfur is used for making clothes.

A mother skunk often picks her babies up in her mouth to carry them to new homes.

The crossbill

Crossbills live in coniferous forests. Males are largely red and black, but females are brown and yellow. They feed entirely on conifer seeds. They often breed in the winter, because there are always plenty of seeds to feed the nestlings.

The crossbill gets its name from its strange crossed beak, which it uses to lever up the cone scales to get at the seeds underneath.

The wood pigeon

Wood pigeons live in and around the deciduous forests of Eurasia. They make soft, cooing calls with the second note very long – *coo-coooo-coo-cu-cu.*

Wood pigeons make flimsy nests with twigs and usually rear three broods in a year. Each brood normally consists of two chicks.

? DO YOU KNOW

Wood pigeons have fast become one of the commonest and most annoying farm pests. They chew the leaves of many crops in the spring and eat a lot of grain in the autumn.

The capercaillie

The capercaillie is a turkey-like bird that lives in the coniferous forests of Eurasia. It eats flowers and berries in the summer, but in the winter it stays in the trees and feeds mainly on pine needles and cones.

CAPERCAILLIE FACTS

- The capercaillie is up to 85 cm long.

- Males gather in forest clearings in the spring to show off their fine tail fans and attract females with a song and dance display.

The great grey owl

The great grey owl lives in the northern forests of Eurasia. It rears up to five chicks in the spring, usually in an old nest of another bird. The chicks can fly by the time they are five weeks old.

GREY OWL FACTS

- The great grey owl is about 70 cm long. It is not as heavy as it looks and is actually quite slim under its thick coat of feathers.

- The owl often hunts by day. It eats mainly lemmings and squirrels.

The sleepy dormouse

Several kinds of dormice live in the woods of Europe and Asia. The one shown below on the right is the hazel dormouse. It is a wonderful climber and lives in thick bushes. It feeds at night on buds, nuts and berries, and insects. Baby dormice are born in leafy nests in the bushes in summer. Dormice sleep all through the winter in cosy nests on or just under the ground.

DO YOU KNOW

The 25–30 cm long fat dormouse is the largest dormouse. It was a favourite food of the Romans. They used to keep the dormice in cages and fatten them up before eating them.

SURVIVAL WATCH

Hazel dormice are now rare because many deciduous woods have been replaced with conifer plantations. They do best in woods that are regularly coppiced, or cut, to produce lots of thick bushes (see page 38).

The European garden dormouse often makes its home in gardens. It steals orchard fruit and also enters houses.

The furry tail is wrapped around the body when the hazel dormouse is asleep. It helps to keep the dormouse warm.

The smelly polecat

The polecat is a cousin of the weasel. It lives in deciduous woods and on farmland in Europe. Also called the foulmart, it can give out a foul smell from glands near its tail.

? DO YOU KNOW

Polecats have been domesticated for a long time. Domestic forms, called ferrets, are usually paler. They are used to catch rabbits.

The beech marten

The beech marten is a sweet-smelling relative of the polecat and is sometimes called the sweet mart. It is up to 80 cm long, including its tail, and is a great climber.

Beech martens live in the deciduous woods of Europe and Asia, but they are also common in and around farms and villages and in the mountains.

The friendly black bear

Black bears live in various parts of the world. Those shown here are American black bears, which live in wooded areas nearly all over North America. They are quite friendly animals and do not attack people unless they are annoyed or injured. But they are a bit clumsy and can cause injuries with their strong claws, so it's not a good idea to get too near to them. Black bears eat just about anything, including nuts, berries, insects, mushrooms and birds, along with mice and other small mammals.

BLACK BEAR FACTS

● American black bears are up to 150 cm long and can weigh 250 kg. Some are actually brown or white.

● Black bears sleep through the winter, but the females wake up for a few days when it is time for them to have their cubs.

Black bears are less common than they used to be, but there are plenty of them in America's national parks. They often beg for food from visitors.

Black bears sometimes catch fish with their mouths or paws, but they don't like the water as much as brown bears.

Black bears are agile climbers and scamper up tree trunks amazingly quickly with the aid of their big, strong claws.

The bears use their powerful feet to dig small mammals from their burrows. They also rip open bees' nests to get honey.

DO YOU KNOW

Black bears are real scavengers. They often empty rubbish bins at picnic sites to find something to eat, and even enter towns and villages to raid the dustbins for scraps.

Two or three tiny cubs are born in a den in the winter. They stay with their mother until they are about six months old.

The grey squirrel

The grey squirrel is an American animal that was taken to England in the 19th century. It gradually replaced the native red squirrel and is now common in most parts of Britain, including parks and gardens. Grey squirrels eat fruits, seeds, fungi and insects. They also eat birds' eggs and they kill trees by eating the bark. They can run up and down tree trunks at great speed.

? DO YOU KNOW

Some types of squirrels are called flying squirrels. Skin stretched between their legs allows them to glide long distances from tree to tree, but they cannot really fly.

The squirrel's bushy tail is used as a rudder when the squirrel leaps from branch to branch.

SQUIRREL FACTS

• Grey squirrels weigh 500 grams and are bigger than European red squirrels.

• Squirrels stay active through the winter, feeding mainly on nuts that they buried in the ground in the autumn.

Neatly split hazel nuts show where squirrels have been eating. They split the nuts with their teeth.

Squirrels lift their food to their mouths in their front paws. Their sharp claws help them to climb easily.

The cunning red fox

The red fox lives in woods and in open country in North America and Eurasia. It eats rabbits and earthworms, and just about every kind of animal in between. When a fox finds a group of rabbits, it may leap up and down and chase its own tail. This seems to mesmerise the rabbits, and the fox then pounces on one of them. Dusk and dawn are the fox's main feeding times.

FOX FACTS

● The red fox is up to 120 cm long, from its head to its tail.

● The male is called a dog fox and the female is called a vixen. The young are called cubs.

The fox's coat is usually a reddish brown, but it may be sandy or even black. Cubs have chocolate-coloured fur.

DO YOU KNOW

Foxes are just as common in towns as in the country. They make their homes in parks and cemeteries and on railway banks, and they find food in dustbins at night.

The bushy tail is called a brush. It is up to 45 cm long and nearly always has white fur at the tip.

Woodland butterflies

Butterflies like sunshine and do not live in really dense woods. They prefer sunny clearings, where there are plenty of flowers to provide the butterflies with sweet nectar. There are some woodland butterflies that can do without flowers. Instead, they drink honeydew – a sugary liquid dropped by tiny insects called aphids.

BUTTERFLY FACTS

● About one-quarter of European butterflies breed in woodlands.

● The purple emperor's caterpillars eat willow tree leaves, but the caterpillars of most woodland butterflies eat low-growing plants.

The European speckled wood (left) likes to bask in the sunshine. It chases other butterflies away from its chosen spot. If its perch becomes shaded, the butterfly flies away to another sunny spot. It feeds mainly on honeydew.

The purple emperor (below) lives in Europe and Asia. The male enjoys drinking from muddy puddles and also from rotting flesh. Butterfly collectors used to tempt this lovely butterfly down from the trees with dead rabbits.

The wings of the male purple emperor have a beautiful purple sheen when they are seen from certain angles.

The purple emperor sucks up nectar and honeydew with a slender tongue, which is coiled up under its head when not in use.

Noisy woodpeckers

Woodpeckers are well named because they spend most of their lives pecking at tree trunks and branches – either to make holes for nests or to get at insects tunnelling in the wood. They have extra-tough skulls so that they don't knock themselves out with all the hammering. About 200 kinds of woodpecker live in the world's woodlands. Most of them eat nuts and seeds as well as insects, but some eat nothing but ants.

DO YOU KNOW

After boring a hole, a woodpecker uses its tongue to drag insects from the wood. Its tongue is so long that it has to be rolled up in the back of the head when not in use.

Green woodpecker

Great spotted woodpecker

Acorn woodpecker

Woodpeckers do not sing. Most of them call to each other by drumming on dead branches. This makes a lot of noise.

Woodpeckers have stiff tail feathers which dig into the bark and help to support the birds while they peck at the trunks.

Acorn woodpeckers make holes in trees and wooden posts, and then wedge acorns in them to form winter larders.

The prickly hedgehog

Hedgehogs are easily recognized by their dense, prickly coats. The western hedgehog shown here lives all over Europe, in fields and towns as well as in woods and hedgerows. It comes out at night and feeds on insects, slugs, worms, and many other small animals. In the autumn it tucks itself up in a nest of dry leaves and spends the winter in a deep sleep called hibernation.

? DO YOU KNOW

If there are hedgehogs where you live, you can tempt them to your garden with some dog food put out at dusk. Give them an occasional treat of bread and milk.

A female hedgehog usually has four or five babies in the summer. They follow their mother everywhere for a week or two. The babies are born without spines, so their mother is not hurt during the birth.

Adult hedgehogs can have about 5000 spines, made from tough hairs – just like the porcupine.

⚡ SURVIVAL WATCH

Thousands of hedgehogs are killed by cars every year, but they still seem to be pretty common. The use of poisonous slug pellets in gardens is a more serious threat to the slug-eating hedgehogs.

A frightened hedgehog can roll up into a prickly ball until its legs and head are completely hidden.

The laughing kookaburra

This Australian bird gets its name from its loud, chuckling call. Kookaburras live in small groups and their calls tell other kookaburras that a particular area is occupied. The calls can be heard at any time of day, but they are especially loud early in the morning – so the kookaburra is also called the alarm bird or breakfast bird.

KOOKABURRA FACTS

● The kookaburra is about 45 cm long.

● It is a kind of king-fisher, but it does not eat much fish. It feeds on lizards, snakes and large insects, as well as the eggs and chicks of other birds.

The kookaburra's original home was in the open woodland of eastern Australia, but it has been taken to many other parts of the continent. It is common in orchards and also in parks and gardens, where it often becomes quite tame.

Kookaburras nest in holes in trees and sometimes in walls and river banks. The parents take turns to sit on the eggs.

The kookaburra usually kills its prey by holding it in its powerful beak and bashing it hard against a branch.

Looking after the woodlands

It seems odd, but we actually have to cut trees down to look after woodland wildlife properly. Not all the trees are felled, of course. Just a small area is cut each year. Most of the trees are cut to ground level, in a process called coppicing. Where the trees have been cut, the extra light allows lots of flowers to grow. These attract insects, and the insects attract birds, so all the wildlife benefits. The cut trees soon sprout again, which means that a coppiced woodland contains trees at all stages of growth.

SURVIVAL WATCH

Millions of trees are dying because of acid rain. Fumes from factories and cars turn rain into weak acids which damage leaves. We must control this form of pollution if we are to save the forests.

The small trunks and branches cut down during coppicing are often used to make fencing. The trees grow up again and about 15–20 years later they are ready for another cut.

Useful words

Antlers The branched bony outgrowths on the heads of male deer. They fall off after the breeding season, but the deer soon grow new ones.

Camouflage The way in which animals hide from their enemies by resembling their surroundings or blending in with them.

Conifer Any tree, such as a pine or a fir, that bears its seeds in cones.

Coppicing The cutting of trees to ground level so that they send up a fresh crop of slender branches.

Cub The name given to a young fox, bear or badger.

Deciduous Deciduous trees are those that drop their leaves in the autumn.

Domesticated Not wild. Domesticated animals are those that have been tamed by people for various purposes.

Eurasia The name given to the land mass that consists of Europe and Asia.

Evergreen Evergreen trees are those that keep their leaves all through the year.

Extinction The dying out of any kind of plant or animal. An extinct creature is one that no longer lives anywhere on Earth.

Gland Any part of the body that makes a substance and then sends it to another part of the body or to the outside to perform a particular job. The defensive sprays of ants and skunks are produced in glands.

Hibernation The long winter sleep of many animals.

Litter The name given to a group of baby mammals that are all born at the same time. The word is also used for the dead leaves on the woodland floor.

Mammal Any member of the large group of animals that feed their babies with milk from the mother's body.

Marsupial Any member of the group of mammals in which the babies are carried in a pouch in the mother's body. Most marsupials live in Australia.

Pest An animal that makes a nuisance of itself by damaging people's crops and other possessions.

Pollution The spoiling of air, water or soil by poisonous substances, including smoke from cars and factories.

Prey Any animal that is caught and eaten by another animal. The hunting animal is called a predator.

Rodent Any member of the mouse and squirrel group of mammals, with chisel-like front teeth that are used for gnawing.

Scavenger Any animal that feeds mainly on dead matter.

Species A species is any one particular kind of animal or plant, such as a kiwi or a koala.

Territory The area in which an animal or a group of animals live, and which they defend against other animals of the same kind.

Index